Matthew Meditates

By Ameshia Arthur, LCSW

ILLUSTRATED BY ANNA ROMANENKO

DEDICATION

To my sweet inspirations.

Matthew is manly.

Matthew is muscular.

Matthew meditates.

Matthew likes mud.

Matthew likes motocross.

Matthew meditates.

Matthew runs marathons.

Matthew fights monsters.

Matthew meditates.

Matthew plays sports.

Matthew gets mad.

Matthew meditates.

Matthew makes slime.

Matthew makes messes.

Matthew meditates.

Matthew mixes.

Matthew molds.

Matthew meditates.

Matthew makes mistakes.

Matthew has a melt down.

Matthew meditates.

Matthew makes chocolate milk.

Matthew is mesmerized by magic.

Matthew meditates.

Why does Matthew meditate?

Matthew is smart.

Matthew is calm.

Matthew is focused because Matthew meditates.

Meditate with Matthew.

Matthew sits on his mat.

Matthew clears his mind.

Matthew takes three minutes to focus on his breathing.

Benefits of meditation

- Improved focus
- Improved memory
- Increased empathy for others
- Improved self esteem
- Increased feelings of calm and relaxation
- Decreases stress

Meditate with your munchkins.

ABOUT THE AUTHOR

Ameshia graduated from San Francisco State University to pursue an elementary school teaching career in high poverty areas. After some time as a teacher, Ameshia realized that before the children and parents could pursue education they would need to have their mental and emotional needs met. With this insight, Ameshia pursued a degree in Social Work at CSU Sacramento. Once Ameshia obtained her Masters of Social Work she worked in a variety of communities. Ameshia found great success in supporting people and helping them gain insight and coping tools. Ameshia's experience in education and social work and love for reading and youth then led her to author children's books. In 2017 Ameshia published her first children's book "Brown Boy Brown Boy What Can You Be?" Followed by "Benjamin the Brave: a story about anxiety" in 2018. Ameshia sees her contribution in children's literature as a natural extension of her helping profession.

Made in the USA
Lexington, KY
20 November 2019